IMAGES
of America

FORT DEVENS

IMAGES
of America

FORT DEVENS

William J. Craig

ARCADIA
PUBLISHING

Published by Arcadia Publishing
Charleston, South Carolina

Printed in the United States of America

Library of Congress Catalog Card Number: 2003115655

For all general information contact Arcadia Publishing at:
Telephone 843-853-2070
Fax 843-853-0044
E-mail sales@arcadiapublishing.com
For customer service and orders:
Toll-Free 1-888-313-2665

Visit us on the Internet at www.arcadiapublishing.com

John Craig, a Concord native with the
47th Infantry, Company G, was processed
through the Union army cantonment at
Groton Junction. (Craig family.)

CONTENTS

ACKNOWLEDGMENTS

While writing this book, many people contributed their knowledge, photographs, and time to assist me in this endeavor. These individuals have shown much kindness and hospitality to a perfect stranger. My sincere appreciation is extended to the following: Beth Barker, Devens Reserve Forces Training Area (RFTA) acting historian; Linda Jeleniewski, former public affairs officer; Mildred Chandler, volunteer at the Freedom's Way Heritage Association; Allen Goodrich, curator at the John F. Kennedy Library and Museum; Walter Chisholm, 45th Infantry Division Museum; and David Butler of www.cromwellbutlers.com. Also, special thanks to my editor, Tiffany Howe, whose persistence was instrumental in this book's publishing. I thank my parents, John and Barbara Craig, for the gift of life and my cousin, author William Craig, whose advice and friendship will always be treasured. Lastly, I thank my wife, Joanne, whose love has always sustained me through good and bad times. Without her enduring love and support, none of this would have been possible.

This book is dedicated to all the U.S. Army personnel who passed through the gates of Fort Devens to answer the call in defense of freedom and never came home or were killed in action. These soldiers are more than a name on a monument. Their memories are seared into the hearts of their families. Winston Churchill once said, "Never has so much been owed to so few by so many." This quote sums up our unpayable debt to these fallen centurions who stood a post to ensure that American liberties continued. They and their families will always be in our prayers.

INTRODUCTION

For nearly 350 years, there has been a military presence in or around the area known as Fort Devens. The earliest military occupation occurred in 1656. Maj. Simon Willard, a colonizer for the British, was ordered to form a colony and establish a garrison for troops on territory known as Nashoba, near the Nashaway River. He settled some 40 households in the area, allocating their land, administering justice, commanding troops, and acting as governor of the Nashoba colony.

Major Willard's house was located at the Verbeck Gate of Fort Devens. This house was not only the residence of Major Willard's numerous families (he was married three times and had 17 children), it was also a meeting place to conduct all colonial affairs in the region. In addition, it served as a military garrison, housing Willard's Dragoons, soldiers of Britain, and the first organized military force west of Boston. In 1676, the house was pillaged and burned by the Niantick Indians, who came down the Mohawk Trail in King Philip's War (1675 to 1676). The entire colony was destroyed, and many of the settlers were slaughtered. A handful of survivors, including Major Willard, fled to Boston and never returned.

Camp Stevens was the next military camp to settle in the area of Fort Devens. Camp Stevens was located at Groton Junction, approximately one mile from the Verbeck Gate. It served as an army cantonment during the Civil War for the 53rd Massachusetts Volunteer Infantry. Camp Stevens closed shortly after the Civil War ended.

In 1915, the War Department began to realize a need for an army camp in the northeast region of the United States, due to the growing conflict of World War I in Europe. The War Department offered to rent land in Shirley, Ayer, Harvard, and Lancaster for a $1.50 a month, with an option to purchase that would expire in 1920. Two hundred and fifty parcels were leased from 112 landlords for the construction of Camp Devens. This site was believed to be ideal due to its close proximity to the Boston & Maine Railroad. This was a necessary factor because of the need to dispatch troops quickly. Edward Richardson, who worked for the War Department and had negotiated the acquisition of the land, suggested naming the post after Major Willard, who had occupied the site 250 years earlier. Since Major Willard had been a British colonizer and not in the U.S. Army, the camp took its name from Civil War brevet Maj. Gen. Charles A. Devens. Devens was a Massachusetts native and attorney general under Pres. Rutherford B. Hayes.

In June 1917, construction began on Camp Devens. The largest workforce ever assembled in the United States converged on the site to build an entire city for 10,000, including infrastructure. The building rate during this time was 10.4 buildings a day.

One

CAMP DEVENS

The post officially opened as Camp Devens on September 5, 1917. It was one of only 16 army cantonments in the country. Two divisions were assigned to the camp: the 76th and the 12th. John B. Murphy of Fitchburg was the first man from New England to report for the 1917 draft. During World War I, more than 100,000 troops were processed and trained at the camp.

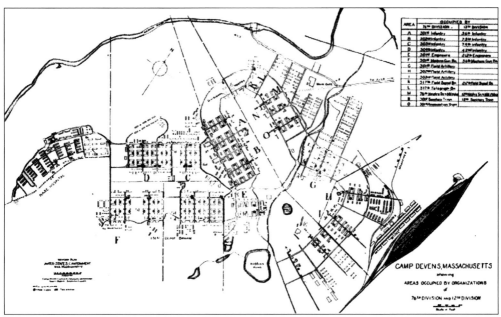

This official map shows the original layout of the post in 1917. Also shown are the areas that were occupied by each organization. The physical layout of the post has changed drastically since this time. (U.S. Army.)

This photograph shows the frenzied building pace that continued into 1918. The building of a cantonment from scratch in the middle of woodlands was a massive undertaking.

This image shows workers completing a barracks building in 1917. These buildings were open-bay barracks that could accommodate more than 150 men.

More than 100,000 troops passed through the original main gate at Camp Devens to begin their military career. In this image, visitors await their family members.

This photograph from 1917 shows the depot brigade. These buildings were usually a flurry of activity. On the left side of the steps, a drill instructor can be seen addressing his platoon of recruits. (Craig family.)

This was the first home of the camp commander Maj. Gen. Harry F. Hodges. He was the first commander and this home's first resident. This home was utilized by eight other commanders until a permanent brick residence was built in the 1930s.

These were the first five buildings of the field hospital. The continuing construction of another hospital building can be seen at the bottom of this photograph. This hospital complex trained the men of evacuation hospital No. 24 before they were sent to France.

A squad of raw recruits dressed in their newly issued uniforms undergoes a semaphore drill. Once learned, this drill allowed these troops to be highly effective with the signal battalion. (Craig family.)

This building was home to the YWCA hostess house. The YWCA was a predecessor of the USO. On Friday and Saturday nights, dances were held here to entertain the troops. (Craig family.)

Physical exercise has always been an integral part of army training. This platoon of recruits is taking part in physical fitness training on the parade field. (Craig family.)

These unassuming buildings were the officers' quarters of the 301st infantry, who were attached to the 76th Infantry Division.

Here, officers at Camp Devens fall out for morning roll call. Officers were housed in single-story buildings with private rooms.

These men of the 76th Infantry Division are raising the flag for morning revelry outside division headquarters. The 76th Infantry was comprised of four infantry battalions, three field-artillery battalions, one machine-gun battalion, one signal battalion, and one telegraph battalion. It also maintained one sanitary train and conducted the headquarters training of the military police.

Recruits are awaiting the call for assembly. The old army adage "hurry up and wait" was true even during World War I.

No matter what time period a soldier may have served, marching has always been an important aspect of military training. This group of soldiers is returning from a hike. (Craig family.)

A lone soldier walks along a road heading away from the 76th Infantry Division encampment at Camp Devens. This camp was located near Cook and Carey Streets.

This barrack was utilized by the 301st Infantry troops. Notice the dirt road and sparse landscaping that surround the building.

James Craig of Concord, Massachusetts, was inducted into the army and trained at Camp Devens. He was sent to the battlefields of Europe and returned to Camp Devens after the war with more than 150,000 other troops to be separated from the army. (Craig family.)

The YMCA occupied these buildings. The YMCA was the first civil social welfare organization to offer its services to the army.

These photographs depict army training at Camp Devens in 1917. Except for the antiquated weapons and uniforms, the training was the same as present-day recruits undergo. (Craig family.)

These photographs show typical scenes around the camp. Notice the troop trucks parked on the street in the center photograph. (Craig family.)

Here are several views of the different buildings that were used by the YMCA. A newly inducted recruit would receive help from the YMCA in countless ways, from sending his civilian clothes home to providing writing paper, postage, educational lectures, athletics, and religious meetings. (Craig family.)

This interior image of a YMCA hut shows troops utilizing the services that were offered to them. These huts were designed to serve as substitute homes, schools, and churches for the troops.

Soldiers stand outside the YWCA auditorium. When new troops arrived, they found the YWCA was ready to help acclimate them to military life.

QUARTERS 36th INFANTRY

HEADQUARTERS 42d INFANTRY

OFFICERS' CLUB

Headquarters, Development Battalions.

Y. W. C. A. Hostess House.

These buildings were used as support facilities for the different division personnel stationed at the post. Each division had its own headquarters in order to process personnel and individualize training. (Craig family.)

The Liberty Theatre was the first post theater at Camp Devens. The theater was a major attraction among the troops seeking relief from the military aspect of their new lives.

This view of Camp Devens was taken from where the water tower is presently located, in a view looking west toward Sherman and MacArthur Avenues.

Its often been said that an army travels on its stomach, and it was true at Camp Devens as well. This image shows the central restaurant on the post. This restaurant was responsible for serving 30,000 meals a day to the permanent personnel.

These buildings housed the horses for the cavalry, as well as the riding equipment

KNIGHTS OF COLUMBUS BUILDINGS

The Knights of Columbus also had a strong presence on the post. They occupied several buildings and helped to keep up the morale of the soldiers. (Craig family.)

LIBRARY

LIBERTY THE

ENLISTED MEN'S CLUB

Red Cross Building.

Red Cross Building.

These buildings helped the troops to fill what little recreation time they had. (Craig family.)

Legend has it that mothers, wives, and sweethearts of troops serving at Camp Devens during World War I brought stones from all over the country to the post. Then, post engineers constructed this monument with the stones and dedicated it on November 23, 1918. (Craig family.)

The 302nd field artillery battalion was located where the permanent brick officer housing on Walnut Street is located today.

This post office was responsible for all the mail that was sent to and from the camp. This was a rather daunting task when considering that the average soldier received three letters a week and sent five letters a week. At any given time, there were approximately 43,000 troops on the post.

This bird's-eye view gives a sense of the enormous size of the camp. At its peak, there were 1,448 buildings; only the quartermaster's building remains today. (Craig family.)

The YWCA provided the first libraries on Camp Devens. By 1918, the army had established a permanent post library. From 1918 to 1996, Fort Devens had a library to promote education among post personnel.

These recruits are participating in mass calisthenics on one of the drill fields. Physical training is an important part of a recruit's indoctrination.

This is a view of the base hospital in 1917. When the influenza epidemic reached Camp Devens, it was devastating. Fourteen thousand troops were stricken with influenza. This hospital and its staff worked around the clock caring for the sick troops. (Craig family.)

It is important to remember that infantry soldiers during World War I also had to be trained as proficient cavalry troops. This photograph shows the remount station. Here, the horses were fed, watered, and allowed to rest until they were needed again. (Craig family.)

These recruits are participating in a Hebert exercise on a drill field. (Craig family.)

These new recruits are learning the first aspect of military life: the proper way to execute a salute.

Due to the nature of trench warfare during World War I, recruits had to learn the proper technique of using a bayonet. These techniques had to become second nature to these men, otherwise their effectiveness on the battlefield would be greatly diminished.

These troops are ready on the firing line. Every army recruit becomes acquainted with his rifle. The rifle has become an important part of army indoctrination.

Here, recruits wait in formation to attempt the bayonet course. The bayonet course is a phase of training that develops alertness and quickness of the body and mind. Many problems are set before the trainee during these exercises.

Originally, drill and ceremony was introduced to the army during the Revolutionary War. Since that time, every recruit has learned "D and C."

These five images show the different aspects of infantry training. Notice the troops going through training with their gas masks on.

Here, a soldier stands guard outside his barracks. (Craig family.)

Capt. Sylvester Benjamin Butler was assigned to the 301st supply train at Camp Devens. Captain Butler attended Yale University and graduated in 1913. In 1917, he left a teaching position to join the army. He rose to the rank of captain in one year. The supply train was sent to France in 1918, three months before the war ended. He became commanding officer of the supply train in December 1918. In 1925, he edited and coauthored a book called *The 301st Supply Train in the World War*. He went on to become superintendent of the Groton school district. The S.B. Butler School of Ledyard was named in his honor. (David Butler.)

It is important to note that soldiers at Camp Devens were not only trained for the front lines, but they were also trained to support personnel. Here are the buildings that housed the school for cooks and bakers.

These single-story buildings were quickly constructed to house battalion support facilities. This building was home to the 304th Infantry headquarters.

Noncommissioned officers of the cadre assemble outside the 303rd Infantry battalion headquarters.

After the war ended in Europe, the troops returned home and were processed out. Camp Devens became a ghost town. This is evident in this image of the 301st field artillery barracks that are now empty.

These buildings were home to the headquarters of the engineers. They were located on the approximate site of the Devens firehouse.

This is the cadre of the 301st supply train at Camp Devens in 1917. (David Butler.)

This was the headquarters of the Citizens Military Training Camp (CMTC). The CMTC program indoctrinated civilian males ages 17 to 27 into military life. On August 9, 1925, students attending the CMTC program assembled in the chapel grove area to dedicate a nondenominational altar. The CMTC program lasted only a short time during the 1920s. The altar, however, remained behind the Crossroads Service Club until it was removed when the post closed in 1996.

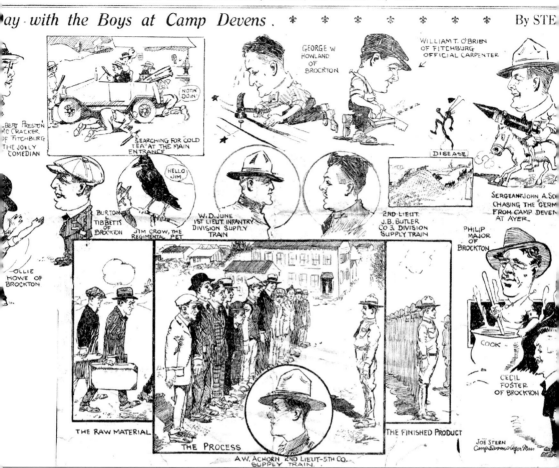

This cartoon from World War I displays a day in the life of recruits at Camp Devens. (David Butler.)

This bird's-eye view shows troops marching in formation between the depot and brigade headquarters at Camp Devens c. 1917. (Fort Devens archive photograph.)

Two

FORT DEVENS
MODERNIZATION

In 1919, the War Department exercised its option to purchase the land the post was on. They purchased the land for $15 an acre. Ironically, this was done one year prior to the end of the lease. All the while, the War Department considered closing the post. Through the efforts of congresswoman Edith Nourse Rogers of Lowell, appropriations were made in 1927 for the permanent construction of buildings on the post.

This structure was one of the first permanent brick buildings erected on the post. It was first known as the infantry battalion barracks. Later, these and the other barracks became classrooms and offices. (Fort Devens archive photograph.)

The 13th Infantry passes in review on Rogers Field in 1928. The 13th Infantry was put in permanent charge of the post in September 1930. (Fort Devens archive photograph.)

This is the headquarters and administration building on Buena Vista Street. This photograph was taken after the building's completion in 1931. Around this same time, the installation's designation was changed from Camp Devens to Fort Devens. (Fort Devens archive photograph.)

Taken in July 1928, this view shows the parking lot of the quadrangle. One of the completed infantry battalion barracks can be seen in the background. (Fort Devens archive photograph.)

Cavalry units parade on Rogers Field. The quadrangle buildings can be seen in the background. Fort Devens had cavalry units stationed there until the early 1940s. This photograph was taken in the early 1930s, prior to the advent of the mechanized infantry. (Fort Devens archive photograph.)

In 1940, the quadrangle buildings were centered around a beautiful courtyard. Within a few years' time, this courtyard would be replaced by a parking lot. (Fort Devens archive photograph.)

From 1933 to 1937, Fort Devens was designated 3rd Civilian Conservation Corps (CCC) district No. 2. One hundred thousand men between the ages of 17 and 26 were processed into the CCC to work on conservation projects. These men were put to work to improve the landscaping at Fort Devens, as well as other projects around the country. They constructed Memorial Circle in 1935, and a plaque commemorating their work was placed there. In this photograph, taken upon completion of the circle, the permanent officer housing can be seen to the right of the circle. (Fort Devens archive photograph.)

In October 1938, a group of soldiers on bivouac discovered what appeared to be a petrified tree. Close examination revealed that it was a concrete structure mocked up to look like a tree. The mock tree was hollow and had an opening at the base to allow a soldier to enter and climb up. This unique item became known as the sniper tree or observation post. It was believed to have been built around World War I. Whether it was made as a training aid or to be used in actual combat is pure conjecture. Sadly, this unique piece of military history broke apart when attempts were made to remove it prior to the post's closing. (Fort Devens archive photograph.)

This view of Rogers Field looks toward the quadrangle. (Fort Devens archive photograph.)

In 1929, Dr. Robert Goddard moved his high-altitude rocket experiments from his aunt's farm in Auburn, Massachusetts, to a remote section of Fort Devens. Dr. Goddard is often referred to as the father of rocketry, and his experiments have been credited with the birth of NASA. In 1963, on Armed Forces Day, a memorial tower was placed on the testing location on Sheridan Road near the Jackson Gate. (Fort Devens archive photograph.)

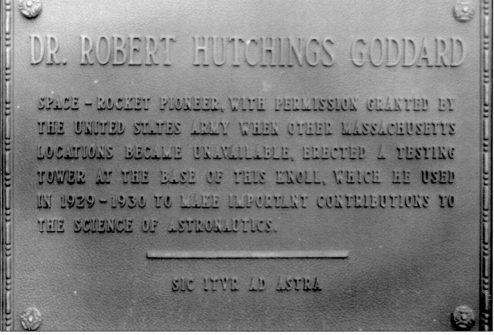

This plaque, along with the memorial tower, was removed on August 17, 1994, when the post began to close. (Fort Devens archive photograph.)

By 1935, most of the original buildings of Camp Devens had been torn down and replaced with permanent brick structures. This image shows the new guardhouse and main gate of Fort Devens.

This is a view of the newly completed, permanent regular army barracks and Rogers Field. Notice the lone car traveling toward the barracks.

This was the permanent brick replacement residence of the post commander.

These town homes were built to house noncommissioned officers and their families. These buildings were in constant use until the post closed.

This building was originally intended to house the post hospital. Shortly after it was completed, base personnel quickly realized that the building was woefully inadequate to handle the personnel needs of the post. So plans were made to build a new hospital complex near the Shirley Gate. The building was then used as the post headquarters annex until the post closed.

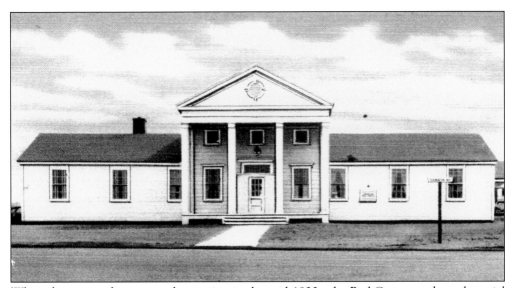

When the post underwent modernization in the mid-1920s, the Red Cross was the only social welfare agency that remained on base after World War I. This image shows the permanent building that was assigned to the Red Cross. There was a representative on call 24 hours a day to assist with emergencies. It is currently occupied by the Harvard Teen Center.

This is the Mirror Lake recreation area. Mirror Lake has a long history of offering family fun to military personnel and their families. Today, Mirror Lake is open to everyone for swimming, boating, fishing, and picnicking.

The sports arena building was originally built to provide a space for post personnel to participate in athletic activities. The building remains today, awaiting a renewed life in the civilian world.

Three

A CENTURY OF CONFLICT

World War I was supposed to be the war to end all wars. By 1940, however, the public came to the realization that the 20th century was soon to become a century of conflict. In 1940, Fort Devens once again became a reception station for thousands of draftees from all over New England. This was due to the institution of the first peacetime draft. At the war's peak, there were 65,000 enlisted men to one officer. During the winter of 1940 to 1941, Theodore Roosevelt Jr. arrived at the post to take his position as commanding officer of the 26th Infantry Regiment.

The men of Company D 26th Infantry ski patrol are seen with a heavy-duty .30-caliber machine gun. From left to right are Cpl. B.E. Casey, Lt. R.S. Case, and Sgt. M.N. Bill on March 11, 1941. (Fort Devens archive photograph.)

With the emergence of air power, the War Department approved construction of Devens Army Airfield, which was completed in 113 days at a cost of $680,000. The airfield became home to the 152nd observation squadron. Pictured here are two L 16 aircraft of the squadron. (Fort Devens archive photograph.)

This is the bridge over the Nashoba River going towards the Shirley Gate. The hospital complex can be seen in the background. In 1944, what became known as the "Fort Devens experiment" occurred at the post hospital. This experiment allowed African American nurses to care for Caucasian soldiers. The experiment was a success, and by 1946, all U.S. army hospitals had desegregated nursing staffs. (Fort Devens archive photograph.)

With the impending onslaught of World War II, the army began construction of hundreds of thousands of temporary barracks, known as T barracks, around the country to house the new recruits. This image portrays a typical company street at Fort Devens.

Within a short period of time, Fort Devens experienced rapid growth. This is evident by this aerial view of the newly constructed barracks.

This is an exterior and interior view of the Crossroads Service Club. This club served as a social and recreational club for enlisted men during what little off-duty time existed.

In July 1940, the first recruit reception station opened at Fort Devens. As the war escalated, so did the need for a larger reception station. And by 1942, this station was closed and the operation was moved to a larger facility on the post.

By May 1942, the reception center was moved once again to its third and final location on the hill near the water tower. During World War II, the reception center processed more than 614,021 inductees between July 1940 and April 1946.

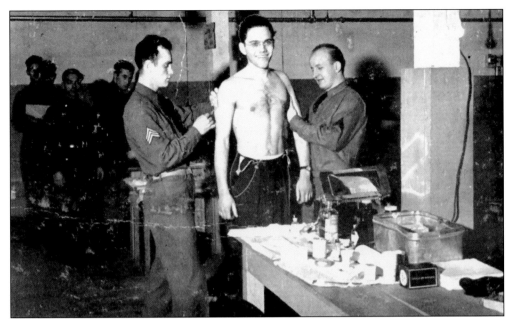

Most, if not all, veterans remember receiving their vaccination shots the first day at the reception station. Here, a new inductee receives his inoculations at the center.

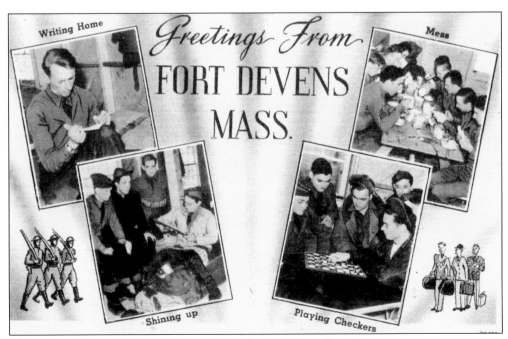

This postcard gives a glimpse of a recruit's daily activities at Fort Devens.

Originally known as post theater No. 1, this theater was later renamed the Bataan-Corregidor Memorial Hall. During World War II, this theater was used to show training films to the troops.

Here, recruits stand in formation for inspection. What former recruit does not remember falling into formation and learning the art of dress right dress?

Recruits pictured here are learning the proper way to make up a rack.

Troops fall out on a cold autumn day to drill as a company on Rogers Field.

This was a common site on company streets at Fort Devens during World War II. These vehicles were referred to as phantom vehicles, but to the GIs, they were just jeeps.

Graduation day was a happy day for recruits in basic training. Here, recruits pass in review at Rogers Field on graduation day.

These ambulances are lined up to participate in a field exercise on the south post. Training of medical personnel in battlefield situations was and still is imperative to the mission of medics in the army.

This is the entrance to the POW camp at Fort Devens in March 1944. This picture is from a film taken by order of U.S. camp commander Colonel Storke. The camp could house 5,000 prisoners. Several escapes took place during its existence. The POWs that were housed on the post were mainly from Rommel's Afrika Corp and were not die-hard Nazis. In fact, 1,391 out of the 3,102 German prisoners voluntarily signed a petition calling on Germany to end the war. Italian POWs were also housed here. The camp officially closed in May 1946. (German Resistance Memorial Center.)

The last of the World War I buildings at Fort Devens can be seen in the background of this photograph. The quartermaster utilized this building until the post was closed in 1996. Here, an unknown soldier leaves with some equipment that was requisitioned to him. In the background, quartermaster personnel are unloading a supply truck. (45th Infantry Division Museum.)

As World War II escalated, so did the build up of military armament and equipment. This former drill field was converted to an artillery storage area. For the second time in the 20th century, Fort Devens became an embarkation point for supplies and personnel heading to England. These men and supplies were not aware that they were about to become part of the largest invasion force in history. D-Day was right around the corner. (45th Infantry Division Museum.)

These troops are members of the 45th Infantry Division on a break from field maneuvers on the south post. The 45th Infantry Division was comprised of National Guard troops from Oklahoma and surrounding states. These men were cowboys, farmers, and Cherokee Indians. During World War II, they saw 511 combat days and eight campaigns. Eight men from the 45th Infantry Division received the Medal of Honor for their actions during World War II. (45th Infantry Division Museum.)

The troops pictured here are part of a convoy that has stopped for a moment on a street in Ayer, just outside Fort Devens. This was a typical scene to the residents of Ayer during the war years. (45th Infantry Division Museum.)

Pictured here are troops of the 45th Infantry Division on a hike through a training field on the south post. Training on the south post consisted of hiking trails, firing ranges, obstacle courses, artillery ranges, bivouac areas, and simulated battlefields. These facilities all helped to prepare the troops for what laid ahead of them. (45th Infantry Division Museum.)

These men are part of a field-artillery squad. They are seen here assembling outside their barracks. They not only had to know how to keep these hungry guns fed, they also had to know how to transport and repair them. (45th Infantry Division Museum.)

Members of the 45th Infantry Division take time to pose for a picture outside their barracks. Men of the 45th liberated Hitler's Munich apartment, his alpine retreat, and the Berlin bunker. Gen. George S. Patton paid these men the highest compliment when he said, "Born at sea, baptized in blood, your fame shall never die, the 45th is one of the best if not actually the best division in the history of American arms." (45th Infantry Division Museum.)

This hospital complex was built to accommodate the post's newly acquired designation of reception station in 1940. It was named the Lovell Army Hospital.

Religion played an important role in the lives of the recruits and troops.

From 1950 to 1954, Fort Devens inducted 85,000 recruits for the Korean War. The most famous inductee during this time was Pvt. Edward M. Kennedy. Private Kennedy served honorably and went on to a successful political career as senator of Massachusetts. (John F. Kennedy Library and Museum archive photograph.)

This is an aerial view of the installation commander's home, located at 1 Buena Vista Street. Thirty seven commanders lived in this stately residence until the post closed. (Fort Devens archive photograph.)

From the time of its construction until the post closed, the administrative offices used this building exclusively.

This is a view of the C Company barracks. This barracks was built in the mid-1950s to accommodate students assigned to the new Army Security Agency (ASA) school that was moved to Fort Devens. (Walter Chisholm.)

VIEW OF REGULAR ARMY BARRACKS,
FORT DEVENS, MASS.

This is a view of Revere Hall, home to the ASA school. This building is now part of the Devens historic district.

This was the main post exchange and cafeteria. Here, a soldier could purchase razor blades, shaving cream, stamps, and postcards to send home. This building was recently torn down to make room for a new shopping complex. (Walter Chisholm.)

The grounds between the barracks were in constant use by ASA students. (Walter Chisholm.)

This is the view of the C Company parking lot. Notice the T barracks are still in use in the background. (Walter Chisholm.)

This is an interior view of the ASA training school barracks in the 1960s. Barracks life has not changed in almost 40 years. (Walter Chisholm.)

This was the KIKBO amateur radio station, also known as MARS. Here, students learned the art of Morse code interception. These students became affectionately known as "ditty boppers." (Walter Chisholm.)

This is another view of ASA students heading to class. (Walter Chisholm.)

From left to right are Claude Hill, Walter Chisholm, Donald Bauman, Ronald Ullerup, Lloyd Vandervolt, Paul Eddy, and Robert Greenhowe. These ASA students take time out for a picture. (Walter Chisholm.)

In November 1950, the ASA was transferred to Fort Devens from Carlisle Barracks in Pennsylvania. The move was completed in April 1951, and it was redesignated the U.S. Army ASA Training Center and School. The school was located in Revere Hall, one of the former battalion barracks. In the picture above, students are on waste-disposal detail. The barrels are marked "classified waste." (Fort Devens archive photograph.)

The reason ASA students are seen marching is due in part to the rule that they were not allowed to drive on base without permission, although students broke this rule any chance they got. (Walter Chisholm.)

ASA students may remember the scuttlebutt that Colonel Millett would take the bayonet off his belt and stick it into the table at staff meetings to emphasize his point during these discussions. (Walter Chisholm.)

In June 1968, military intelligence built a mock Vietnamese village on the post. They staffed it with men of Hawaiian descent. These men were called Menehunes. Their role was to play the Vietcong at this tactical training center. This elaborate village was set up to train army

intelligence officers on the proper procedures in dealing with the villagers. These men are members of the Menehune Platoon Company A. (Fort Devens archive photograph.)

These men dressed in Colonial uniforms posed as members of the Continental Army. Regular army personnel would dress in these uniforms and participate in Colonial reenactments throughout New England. Many personnel considered this skate duty because the members never received any extra duty due to their participation in this unit. (Fort Devens archive photograph.)

Members of the 10th Special Forces Group rappel from a helicopter onto Rogers Field. Scenes like this are a distant memory today. This was part of their STABO training. (Beth Barker.)

Four

FAMILY LIFE AT FORT DEVENS

It is important to remember that Fort Devens was more than a military installation; it was also home to military families. Fort Devens was a self-contained community. There were schools, churches, social clubs, organized sports, and recreation areas and youth activities. All these services were provided by the U.S. Army so as to give the families of Fort Devens a sense of community.

This is an interior view of the E-7-8-9 Club. This was an annex for the NCO club. It was located on the outskirts of Mirror Lake. (Fort Devens archive photograph.)

This was the officers' open mess. It was located on the south side of Rogers Field. The open mess contained a large dinning room and snack bar (which was also known as the Rathskellar), and it had a barbershop, bar, package store, and dusk and satellite rooms that acted as function rooms. This club was also in charge of an 11-room officers' guesthouse. (Fort Devens archive photograph.)

This is the interior view of the post education center. This center was located next to the main post library on Quebec Street. The center provided facilities for self-study groups, college correspondence courses, and general education diplomas. (Fort Devens archive photograph.)

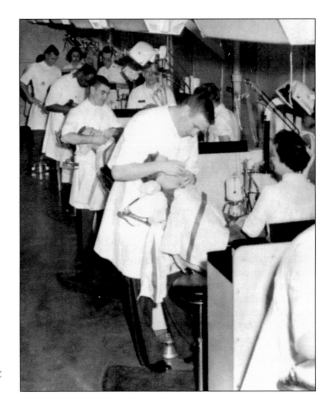

Fort Devens had three dental facilities. Due to the post's remote location, the army authorized the establishment of dental facilities for post personnel and their families. (Fort Devens archive photograph.)

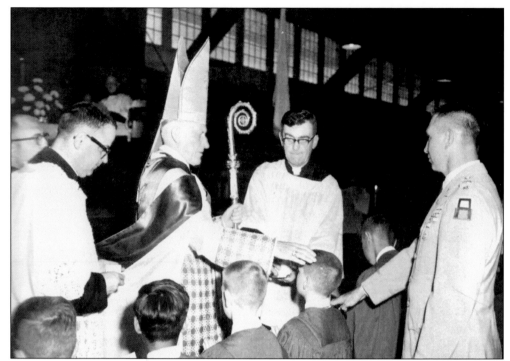

Cardinal Cushing is seen here conducting a Confirmation ceremony at the sports arena building. (Fort Devens archive photograph.)

There were 10 chapels on the post that served the Protestant, Jewish, and Catholic communities. The Jewish Chapel Center, located on Cavite Street, featured a daily noon kosher meal for Jewish personnel. Pictured above is a rabbi celebrating a Jewish High Holy Day. (Fort Devens archive photograph.)

Maj. Gen. William J. Verbeck, post commander from 1959 to 1963, chats with PTA officials. The main gate at Fort Devens was named in his honor. (Fort Devens archive photograph.)

For children ages four to six there was a post kindergarten located in the hospital area. It had four teachers, four classrooms, and room for 115 children. (Fort Devens archive photograph.)

The Fort Devens elementary school was located on the corner of MacArthur and Antietam Streets. This school housed 400 students in grades one and two and 10 teachers. (Fort Devens archive photograph.)

This is an interior view of the post exchange. The main post exchange was located at Quebec and Pine Streets. It had one retail store and seven branch retail stores. They had one cafeteria, 15 snack shops, two mobile snack trucks, seven barbershops, one beauty shop, four laundry and dry-cleaning shops, one radio-television repair shop, three ice-cream trucks, one gasoline service station, and a four-seasons shop for hardware, toys, and garden supplies. (Fort Devens archive photograph.)

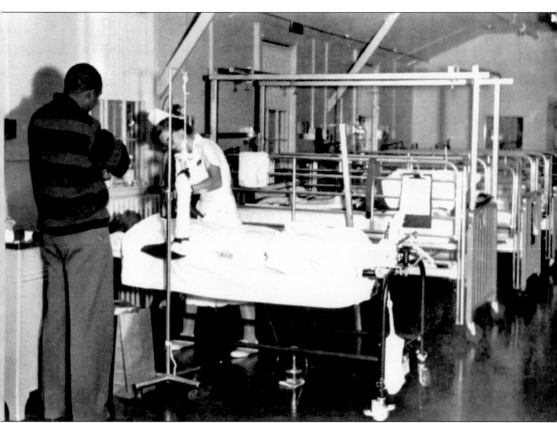

This was the recovery ward at the post hospital. This facility had four operating rooms, 10 wards, and 62 private rooms and could accommodate 200 patients. (Fort Devens archive photograph.)

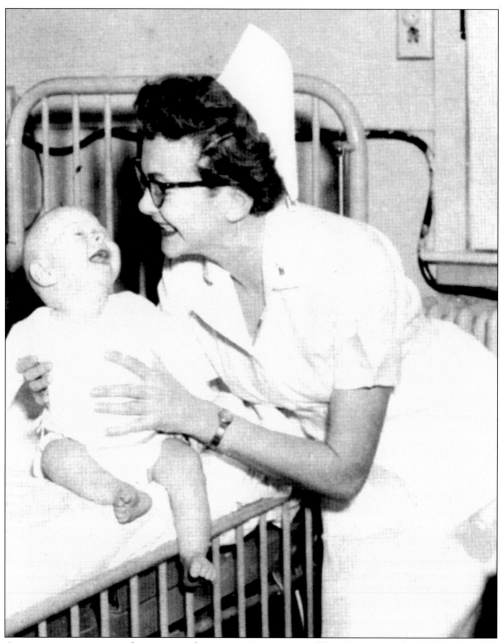

An army nurse seems to be enjoying her patient's company. (Fort Devens archive photograph.)

A member of the Fort Devens basketball team attempts to gain possession of the ball. (Fort Devens archive photograph.)

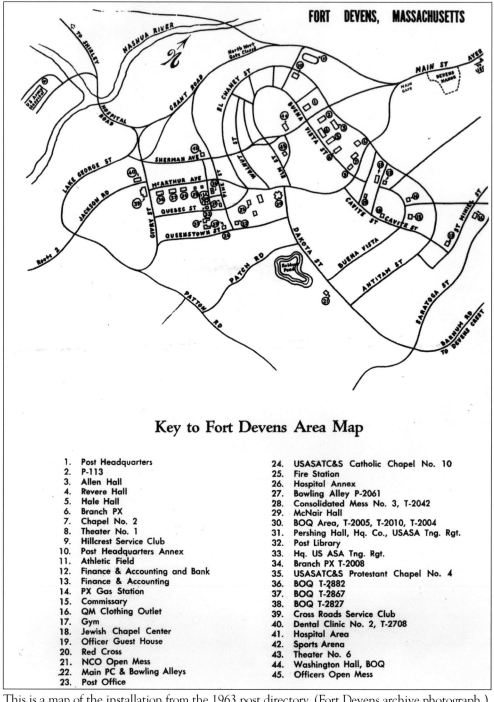

Key to Fort Devens Area Map

1. Post Headquarters
2. P-113
3. Allen Hall
4. Revere Hall
5. Hale Hall
6. Branch PX
7. Chapel No. 2
8. Theater No. 1
9. Hillcrest Service Club
10. Post Headquarters Annex
11. Athletic Field
12. Finance & Accounting and Bank
13. Finance & Accounting
14. PX Gas Station
15. Commissary
16. QM Clothing Outlet
17. Gym
18. Jewish Chapel Center
19. Officer Guest House
20. Red Cross
21. NCO Open Mess
22. Main PC & Bowling Alleys
23. Post Office
24. USASATC&S Catholic Chapel No. 10
25. Fire Station
26. Hospital Annex
27. Bowling Alley P-2061
28. Consolidated Mess No. 3, T-2042
29. McNair Hall
30. BOQ Area, T-2005, T-2010, T-2004
31. Pershing Hall, Hq. Co., USASA Tng. Rgt.
32. Post Library
33. Hq. US ASA Tng. Rgt.
34. Branch PX T-2008
35. USASATC&S Protestant Chapel No. 4
36. BOQ T-2882
37. BOQ T-2867
38. BOQ T-2827
39. Cross Roads Service Club
40. Dental Clinic No. 2, T-2708
41. Hospital Area
42. Sports Arena
43. Theater No. 6
44. Washington Hall, BOQ
45. Officers Open Mess

This is a map of the installation from the 1963 post directory. (Fort Devens archive photograph.)

Five

FORT DEVENS TODAY

During the deployment of troops for operation Dessert Storm and Dessert Shield, 3,000 reservists and guardsmen were also deployed from Fort Devens. This deployment made it apparent that the U.S. Army was undergoing yet another change. No longer would they require massive amounts of troops and logistical support. The United States was now the most powerful nation, due in part to the collapse of the Soviet Union. The army had seen the future, and with the advent of stealth aircraft and smart bombs, they could scale down their operations. The future was the reliance of the army on the citizen soldier. In 1991, Fort Devens was placed on the base closure list. On March 31, 1996, in a ceremony conducted by the U.S. Army, the post officially closed.

Training continued at Fort Devens for the next five years, only the troops were slowly decreasing in number. (Fort Devens archive photograph.)

Army reserve troops undergo amphibious training on the Nashoba River. (Fort Devens archive photograph.)

A loaded Huie chopper gets ground clearance for take off at a training area in the south post. (Fort Devens archive photograph.)

The post administration building overlooks the official closing ceremonial proceedings with an uncertain future. For nearly 80 years, the U.S. Army has had a military presence in New England, the birthplace of the American militia. With the closing of Fort Devens came the closing of a chapter in American history. (Fort Devens archive photograph.)

These housing units are slated for demolition. This is due to the exorbitant cost to delead and rehabilitate the properties. Mass Development has decided to ecologically clean up not only the structures, but also the soil these buildings occupy. (Craig family.)

The Fort Devens cemetery was dedicated in 1939. Thirty graves were transferred from the original Camp Devens cemetery, as well as ninety seven graves from several fort cemeteries in Boston Harbor. Twenty two German POW graves and five Italian POWs are interred here from World War II. Soldiers and sailors of six of America's wars are buried here. (Craig family.)

The former Fort Devens historic area has become a popular destination for former army veterans. Pictured here is Joseph Falzone. Falzone enlisted in the U.S. Army in 1942 and did his basic training at Fort Devens. Since that time, he has become a prolific songwriter. He composed the song "Ode to Massachusetts," which has become the official ode of the commonwealth. (Craig family.)

Originally, this building was the post stable. Forty horses were housed here for the cavalry; there was also a hayloft in the attic of the building. Prior to the post's closing, this building was the post museum, which housed over 3,000 artifacts pertaining to New England's military history. It is the present home of the Native American Cultural Center. (Craig family.)

On the corner of Queenstown Street is this former theater. The floor and seats have been removed. Telephone equipment is now stored within the building. This theater was built in the early 1940s and was in continuous use until the early 1990s. (Craig family.)

On the right of this photograph is a former dining hall that has been boarded up. These buildings were the first to be cleared out by the army during the closure proceedings. Since being abandoned, they have not only been vandalized, but have also structurally deteriorated to the point of being unsafe. (Craig family.)

An interior view shows a dining hall located within the former temporary barracks area. Each training area had its own dining hall centrally located near the barracks and company headquarters. Each dining hall served approximately 3,000 meals a day at the height of activity. (Craig family.)

This area, now overgrown and dilapidated, was once a flurry of activity. These former World War II barracks were originally meant to be used for the temporary housing of troops. They ended up being used for more than 50 years. The third and final location of the recruit reception center happens to be the last remaining area of T barracks. Soon, this area will be demolished due to the unsafe condition of these buildings. (Craig family.)

This is an interior view of the first floor of a T barracks. These barracks were built all around the country during World War II. Notice the central heat and air-conditioning vent that was added later to modernize this building. (Craig family.)

This is the Bataan-Corregidor Memorial Hall, also known as theater No. 1. This theater had two performances nightly and a matinee for children on Saturday afternoons. It was also used to show training films. (Craig family.)

An interior view of the Bataan-Corregidor Memorial Hall theater is depicted here. This theater is currently awaiting a renewed life. It resides in the historic district of the former post and, hence, it cannot be torn down. (Craig family.)

This unusual looking fire truck is a converted military Deuce and a Half. Notice the canvas roof covering the cab. This fire tanker is an original piece of fire equipment that was used by the army. It is currently housed at the Devens fire station. (Craig family.)

This is the Whitemore Service Command Shop. It was completed in 1941 and had the distinction of being the largest repair shop in the world. This facility is still owned by the army, but it is currently closed down. (Craig family.)

These former officer homes, which are on Walnut Street, are in the historic district. Mass Development has rehabilitated these homes and is now offering them for sale to the public. (Craig family.)

An interior view of the living room of one of the former officer's units on Walnut Street shows how it has been remodeled. These units have an asking price in the range of $200,000 to $300,000. (Craig family.)

This is the main gate to Devens Reserve Forces Training Area (Devens RFTA) on Queenstown Street. Each automobile entering must undergo a 100 percent identification check. Security has been heightened since the terrorist attacks of September 11, 2001. (Craig family.)

Formerly, this building housed the headquarters of the 36th medical battalion. It currently is the headquarters of Devens RFTA. (Craig family.)

This is an interior view of the conference room at the headquarters building of Devens RFTA. The walls of this room are covered with photographs of the former Fort Devens commanders and sergeant majors. (Craig family.)

This is a section of wooden pipe that is on display in the conference room of the headquarters building of Devens RFTA. During the construction of Camp Devens in 1917, 81,840 feet of this pipe were used. This original piece of pipe is in remarkable condition and is a wonderful piece of U.S. Army history. (Craig family.)

Two field artillery cannons stand watch over Devens RFTA. A small U.S. Marine force is also headquartered within Devens RFTA. (Craig family.)

This is a portrait of WO Douglas F. Moore of Ayer, Massachusetts. On May 22, 1969, Moore was killed in action in Vietnam. When Fort Devens closed, so did Moore Army Airfield. Devens RFTA area dedicated a former barracks on September 22, 1997, in Moore's honor. The former barracks was renamed Moore Hall and currently houses Devens RFTA administrative offices. (Craig family.)

This is the maintenance parking lot for the Devens RFTA on Queenstown Street. All the former motor-pool facilities are now under the direction of Devens RFTA. (Craig family.)

This view shows the golf course from Bulge Road. Originally built for military personnel, today this course is open to the public. Part of the original course was demolished to make way for the federal medical facility. A new addition to the course was built on a former barracks area. Today, golfers play through tree-lined areas with barracks foundations on the outskirts of the green. (Craig family.)

This is one of three buildings that remain from the former World War II POW camp. These buildings are badly decaying and have remained abandoned for many years. Plans are underway to rehabilitate these buildings so that they may house the future Fort Devens Museum. The Freedom's Way Heritage Association is undertaking to open this museum. (Craig family.)

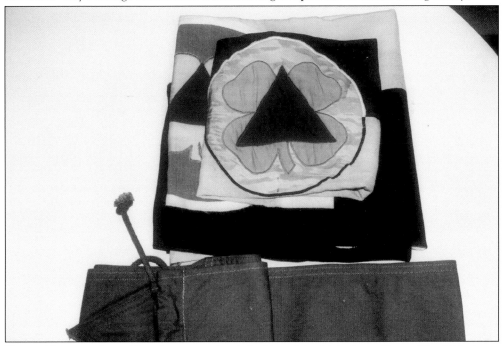

Pictured here are the guidon, banner, and stakeholder of the 13th Army Corps. The 13th Army Corps was activated on January 2, 1958, at Fort Devens and was inactivated on June 5, 1970. A retired Vietnam veteran, Mast. Sgt. Rudolph F. Polzer, donated these items to the Fort Devens Museum. (Craig family.)

These buildings located at Moore Army Airfield are currently being used by the army reserve. The state police are using the main runway for their driving instruction school. (Craig family.)

This is the former entrance to Moore Army Airfield. This facility was once in constant daily use; now it sits in quiet isolation. (Craig family.)

Rogers Field remains unchanged from the time of its military use. It has, however, found renewed life as a soccer field for local and statewide tournaments. (Craig family.)

Looking across Barnum Road, a line of military Humvees is visible. This fenced compound is part of the Massachusetts Army National Guard installation. (Craig family.)

Once a hub of activity, the gate to the south post is now quiet during the weekdays. The south post was acquired in 1942. It is located across Route 2 from the Jackson Gate. The army took the property by eminent domain. The farm families that were located here had 10 days to vacate. The location was chosen because of the proximity of Ordway Railroad Station so that ammunition could be moved by rail from Boston without incident. Fifty ammunition bunkers were built for storage, as well as other training facilities. Located in the vicinity of Whitemore Hill in the infantry assault area is a memorial dedicated to Luther Burbank, a famed horticulturist who was born on the approximate site of the memorial. Currently, the U.S. Army retains possession of the site and the Air Force maintains a radar station in the northwest corner of the post. In 50 years, if the military no longer needs the site, it will revert to the Oxbow Wildlife Refuge. (Craig family.)

Scenes like this have become commonplace around the former installation. Construction crews are working at a feverish pace renovating the former installation. Housing units on Birch Circle, Beech Street, Plum Street, and Locust Street have been torn down. The buildings along Perimeter Road, Gorgas Street, and Lovell Street have been demolished as well. The historic district and the Devens RFTA area are the only buildings that will remain of the former post. Mass Development has done a wonderful job preserving and bringing economic stability to the area. Some people, however, cannot help but wonder if more preservation could have taken place, rather than urban renewal. (Craig family.)

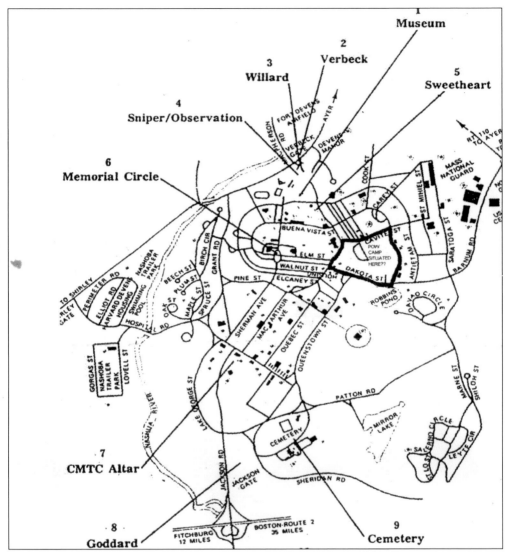

1 Museum

2 Verbeck

3 Willard

5 Sweetheart

4 Sniper/Observation

6 Memorial Circle

7 CMTC Altar

8 Goddard

9 Cemetery

This is a map of the former post showing the approximate location of the post monuments prior to closing. It is important to remember that the army, as part of closure proceedings, removed many of these monuments. The roadways have also been altered since the closing.

FOLLOWING UNITS DEPLOYED FROM FORT DEVENS
WORLD WAR I

76TH DIVISION
12TH DIVISION
26TH DIVISION
25TH ENGINEER REGIMENT
33D ENGINEER REGIMENT
602D ENGINEER REGIMENT
VETERINARY HOSPITAL #1
EVACUATION HOSPITAL #24
BASE HOSPITAL #7
BASE HOSPITAL #76

These plaques are on permanent display near the flagpole on Rogers Field. They are a constant reminder of why Devens remains hallowed ground to the men and women who were once

FOLLOWING UNITS DEPLOYED FROM FORT DEVENS
WORLD WAR II

1ST INFANTRY DIVISION
32D INFANTRY DIVISION
45TH INFANTRY DIVISION
26TH INFANTRY DIVISION
VI CORPS HEADQUARTERS
71ST FIELD ARTILLERY BRIGADE
68TH COAST ARTILLERY REGIMENT
4TH AMPHIBIOUS ENGINEER BRIGADE
366TH INFANTRY REGIMENT

stationed here. (Fort Devens archive photograph.)

It is important to remember that this installation and its personnel played an important role in the history of the United States. These soldiers came to Fort Devens to stand as a deterrent to those who threaten our way of life; just as the embattled farmers and Minutemen once stood on similar ground to end tyranny. Gen. George Washington once stated that "War must be carried on systematically, and to do it you must have men of character activated by principles of honor." This quote seems to summarize the qualities that were possessed by and instilled in every soldier that passed through Fort Devens. These qualities can still be found in the soldiers that presently garrison Devens RFTA. A tradition of duty, honor, and country will continue well into the 21st century. (Fort Devens archive photograph.)